OUT OF THE \

Robin Perry has written an abundance of poetry, which has been regularly published in competition anthologies like the Cleveland *Write Around* since 1989. He won a first prize in that publication in 1991 and a first prize in *World Wide Writers* magazine in 1998. He has also written articles on travel and ornithology. *Out of the Wild* is a collection of Robin Perry's wildlife poems, successfully bringing together his interests in poetry, travel and the natural world.

OUT OF THE WILD
A SELECTION OF WILDLIFE POEMS

Robin Perry

ARTHUR H. STOCKWELL LTD
Torrs Park Ilfracombe Devon
Established 1898
www.ahstockwell.co.uk

British Library Cataloguing-in-Publication Data.
A catalogue record for this book is available
from the British Library.

ISBN 978-0-7223-4026-4
Printed in Great Britain by
Arthur H. Stockwell Ltd
Torrs Park   Ilfracombe
Devon

Contents

Sooty Shearwater

A still, silent glass of milk,
unshaken by hand or breeze.
No boat distorts your image
for long, or timeless song
of peace before September storm.

Sudden, fast, low over glass,
a dark, stiff form drifts in:
no effort costs him rest.
He pauses, scanning surface life,
and surges by strong beat and turn.

He bends a body deftly
with steady, measured shift.
No secrets as pale, light rivers
show beneath his wings like lines
lost on Nazca's rubric plain.

He sees me watching –
a small spectator lost in awe.
Once again he turns, his story fled
with him over slag rock top
as gulls muse idly his gliding course.

Nightjar

Night firms a sweaty grip,
a palm soaking paper into pulp;
the grey heathland cake
of gorse and hawthorn scrub
spreads laced with Nordic birch;
the lattice silver, grey and green,
falls prey to noiseless entropy.
The alien's not yet shown.

Hushed whispers of awe
ripple a chill huddle;
humans hunched with glasses
and flash swaying at each stir.
It's abeyance time, a test
of nerve, patience and sharp bites –
who'll brave it through the raw maw
of early June's damp dusk?

Suddenly a void beyond this night
opens behind an angled birch
scarred by stormy wars.
A sound electric from before this time
whirrs across the slated gloom.
Nature's voice is paused.

A large black moth perhaps?
Or a bat with orange gape
and dark, soulless eyes that know?
It swerves, then flips a course
over flinching bush.
A white flash passes by, still,
then a whipcrack of authority
finally subdues the night.

The time of hush fades out
across the spellbound heath;
the coffin of night's life
seals its lid; the wake ends.

Meerkat

"We know this waterhole,"
I said, directly.
My paw touched Ti's side
with affection.
"Baobabs on the right –
that log the termites own for nest."

I lifted on back paws,
whiffing the evening dust-air
of Kalahari's pan.
"I sniff cat out there –
sharp, foul destroyer
of all that's good."

Tiba, of friendly eyes,
trusts group-scent, and needs
shared wisdom to move.
"How are you so sure?"
Out here is wild-waste
and little cover."

"I smell from air-breath rising,
I see the branch with fur-strand,
I know their season's move."
Ritsa barked dissent.
"Too many fights have turned
your nose into heels."

Angry, I gloved his ear.
"Then try this challenge,
rogue pup of white bum-fur!"
Head drooping, he licked his flank,
sidling sadly to the centre –
safe from tooth-duels.

My eyes danced fondly
round the pack, leg-sore from trekking.
We needed water, grubs, snake
and hill defence.
Behind this face the sorrow
of lost comrades in past fights.

There was a stir –
low snarl out of scrub and stump.
Large buff form speared out
looking for night-feast.
We knew the drill and parted
like the big sea into sky.

This cat had no stomach
for the hunt, and melted
in mirage of sand and sun.
Behind a baobab lay clues
of tail and claws.
Suddenly, all life relief had gone.

We grouped our ranks
and keened late sundown
at no-more-time for a friend.
I caressed the tail and scented.
"She was one of ours.
It's right to say goodnight."

The Blackbird

By the seventeenth century
the blackbird was emerging
like a dawn gipsy through mist.
He flew his forest hideout
and rehoused family and friends
into decent urban homes.

In the nineteenth century
the blackbird had captured
Prague, Paris, London – most of Europe.
He crossed borders, sealed towns
and paraded his colours from trees,
towers, roofs of fine hotels.

No armies have been successful
in stalling his victory course;
no invader ideology
has stemmed his pact with song.

(With apologies to *The Book of Laughter and Forgetting* by
Milan Kundera)

Wallcreeper

Pink butterfly
of crevices,
I looked for you
grubbing quietly
for the living.
Castles and quarries
didn't throw you up –
nor displaying flight
against the snow.
Like you, I fly
erratic through
a world of larvae;
I probe for life
in dead city rocks.

Villanelle: Leven

Where the silent river gouged its way
through conspiracies of trees,
here dark dippers forage the day.

I sometimes left, slipping the fray
for active birds and humming bees
where the silent river gouged its way.

Glimpsing a kingfisher flit away
from sunken branches like sagging knees,
here dark dippers forage the day.

I came to sit, reflect and pray
for griefs at home and overseas,
where the silent river gouged its way.

Often a sheep would come to say
that the grass of life was rich and free –
here dark dippers forage the day.

On days of sadness when down, astray
I went there, camera hugging my knees
where the silent river gouged its way –
here dark dippers forage the day.

Arctic Spring

As the slender hawk owl
glides its journey back,
branch from pine to birch
and on to frozen ditch,
so peered through slit horizon eyes
you glimpse the first sad tears
of snow drop from a twig;
the stronger strengthening
of yellow light, and life's
new bold impulse in
every limb that stretches out.
Drawing back the tundra
tablecloth, the banquet
setting reveals its mammal fare
and puppet jack snipes
crouched down to display defiant
their own horse-gallop high
into thin mid-air,
mating spring to birth.
May days unlock awake
the dawning doors
from Arctic drama's torpor.

Nature's History

Ptolemaic heroes have been
and now lie deep in tombs
beyond the hands of trade and war.
With no witness of a tribe
to recall brave missions
to the centuries' changing children,
pale asphodels alone
nod out a silent tale
and bold-chested stonechats
pound out their song
through new dynasties of life.
New tourist soldiers venting their march
do not comprehend such codes
played out still and yet before them.

Villanelle: The Forest Mood

Varied are the moods of forest landscape
through densest thickets and over the leas;
the hand of Creation forms every shape.

Scarlet crossbills enact their daily rape
of fir cones shattered in the winter breeze;
varied are the moods of forest landscape.

The squirrel, springing like a Barbary ape,
admires the acorns and gratefully sees
the hand of Creation forms every shape.

The emerging adder will casually drape
a tail, displaying without charge or fees;
varied are the moods of forest landscape.

At dusk the replayed nightjar tape
lures in the quarry over bush and trees;
the hand of Creation forms every shape.

The summer rolls in with jaunty jape;
from crooning frogs and eager bees;
varied are the moods of forest landscape,
the hand of Creation forms every shape.

Sketches of Winter

Gatherings of weary people
for early bargains or late
in carol deliveries.

Sad, tearing icicles
fingered down a pipe,
pointing to future freeze-up.

Two rival robins dropping
ritual divisions to hunt
for ice-cracked seeds.

Early great tits calling
their 'teacher' with no yen
to learn from winter ways.

Out on fine-frosted slabs
two pensioners unwilling skate
to opening doors of safety.

Through steaming windows
imperfect candles glow,
shading out impressionist shapes.

Inside draughty living rooms
the tones of croaking coughs
claw back the sense of joy.

A rapid thaw of whitened fields
permits grey lakes over green
and swells the fearful floods.

Along country lanes and bends
cars aquaplane uncertain paths
for carefree, captive drivers.

A gathering-in of darkness
clouds over a sleeping world –
snow falls staccato, still.

Genesis 18: 22–33

They fenced around
the reed bed, confining
those rubbish rushes
that soon must be removed.
The special site, they said,
though of international interest,
was long past
its sell-by date. Besides,
it had been allowed
to become dirty, unkempt
by the managers and staff
and was such an awful site.

They didn't see
one of the last of
a fast-diminishing breed
crane up its slim head
in the shape of a pitiful 'I'.
He had moved in
just two years ago,
homeless, from other beds,
hoping this time
this one would be his.

There are only
fifty of them left –
buff-bodied boomers
site-dwelling in our land.
Suppose fifty are found there,
then fewer and fewer,
till only ten –
will they save our dirty, unkempt land?

The Loss of Land

The fool fettled sandcastles
for foundation to breed
and feed his poor progeny seed;
the wise pragmatist weighed particles
of rock structures, wielding
tools, shielding out floods
from the tent of folly;
and yet rock grumbles, crumbles
against sea's venting fury,
land caving, graving proud homes
to early doom, tombs down;
and yet rock becomes sand
washed into estuary silt,
slipping, sliding like homes built on rock.

Time's finger points out rock into sand,
wisdom to folly and the sad loss of land.

Hobby

Two seconds
of your aerial power
turning and dashing to cover
across my route
with that white-patched face
and hint of red on the shanks.
Dark your form and more,
for what you had to quarry
now yielded to your 'kek'
of fruitful triumph.
On my journey I move
within a space and time.
Your movements onward have redefined
this sense of time by power.

Quail

'Kwitterkik' –
or how fast
the crumbling earth
kicks me along,
the little ones,
so fluffy brown,
so dainty,
trailing all
my movements
as I veer
and steer
the muddied furrows
beyond rumbling machines
or slashing scythe,
nearing,
leering in sunlight –
and suddenly
out of the field
to hedge semi-safety,
my family intact.

Swifts

Gathering again in schools,
they encircle roofs whose gutter nooks
their nests for past three months –
dating, feeding, mating, breeding by air,
screeching out joy in dusk vitality.

Swifts are heading off south –
first followers by night the fly routes
of old Severn and Trent
to cliff-top jetties overlooking the sea
and launch pads to Africa.

The Cuckoo

A once proud stealer
of home care is vanishing,
losing his way to those places
he knew and left others to love.
Briefly now, he seems to call
and slip away eccentrically
down canal pathways
trekking the reed beds' waiting nests,
or on grubbing missions
as though really busy
in sparse sub-Lapland birch scrub.
That yellow-ringed eye stares absently,
hiding purpose and poise;
maybe he has stared at
too many puffs from rifles
floating his way; or the grip
of a gin, wrenching the ankles
of unwary fellows.
Condemned they are
to the early robbery of their life
after they booted out others,
who in turn must die.

FOUR HAIKUS: ON WADING BIRDS

Purple Sandpiper

August they fly back,
purple probers of rock weed
grubbing through the tides.

Whimbrel

The striped crown betrays
their landing with their titters
to whelk-feast the beach.

Curlew

Their plaintive bubble
haunts across lonely bleak moors,
over foulest bog.

Snipe

Long-billed mud-searcher
sniping away near reed beds
when the coast is clear.

Winter Lake

The lake is a skidpad
of frosted ice, log-thick
under a mirror night sky,
each star twinkling
its polar cheer
to a suffering audience
of stony ducks and gulls.
As morning calls
the late dawn *appel*
runs through the roll-call
of living and dead.
Last night's casualty
was a gull, immobile,
marbled to an early death.
Now he stands like
a vigilant sentry,
fixed to a pedestal,
till ice succumbs to water
and stiff-winged statuettes
stir sleeping wings to life.

FOUR HAIKUS: ON THE MOORS

I

They wait in cabins,
shooters of low-flight chancers,
taking no chances.

II

Eager grey phantom
threatens their midday pickings
with menacing drops.

III

Angry shots ring out
protesting such intrusion
from rival bidders.

IV

The harrier drops
once again – to early death
staining pink heather.

Poles

Pearls of snapping ice
that open and close much wider
with each passing solstice
will lose what was theirs –
a pristine freshness,
sharp-coloured focus
in the blazing cold.
Slowly, then quickening,
that peak intensity
slips down and away
like floes to the open sea,
lost in a molten mass
of greyed insipidity;
sunlight will not save this furore.

All Our Days Were Here

It's tricky out here
in the rainy season
when the bridge gets
washed away and roads
better serve boats.
We see more fish
than plants these days,
and when the water's gone
the silts stain brown
those pinks and yellows.
Even on hills
water creeps on up
like a rising tide
that old walls can't stop.
They say it will get worse
and we'll have to live
upstairs many days
or even move away.
Our family were always here
near the paddy fields
and mangrove swamp:
all our days were here.

Urban Spread

The fight is on
to keep these bands and strips
from turning into islands
and even thin-fingered atolls
surrounded by seas
of brick and satellite dish.
For only so long
will the fox and badger
trundle narrowed trails
where harsh harbour
and harvest turn equally rare.
Now squashed remains
and spared tails
are testimonies of the rash
in their daily rush from havens
they don't really need.

The Message

A line bisecting our planet
to and fro:
if you step one way,
it's protection and nurture;
if you step the other,
it's plunder and nemesis.

A meeting to discuss issues
of dire survival:
if it succeeds,
we can move on to conserve;
if it fails,
we fall back on destruction.

A dove flying outside city walls,
offering hope –
but will anyone notice
the quietest message
or turn to the raven
feasting dead flesh?

Axis Shift

Ice clung on late
this year,
not permitting the earth
to breathe
and see Creation's slow
initiation.
Birds took extra-long
to crack
that all too hard surface
for iced worms
and lean squirrels found no solace
in granite nuts.
Talking over these days outside
we used to joke
that the earth had shifted its axis
and swung everything back.

Even spiders' webs hesitate to shed
their frosty silk cocoons
to worlds where days' losses
may spin and fix for ever.

Hare

Long-eared statues immovable,
though wind and rain hurtles
round, encircling, boxing them;
still they stand immovable,
just sometimes punching the air
at invisible enemies.
Rapacious fox, empty-paunched,
jumps the smooth-haired back
of a slow unfortunate,
trying to turn him to ground.
He is left laconic, chewing hair
as consolation for wasted energy.
The prey moves up two gears
and glides through grass
with the skill of charioteers
leading the pack, leaving the fray.
Back on a mound he stands,
resuming his winter pose,
awaiting the lengthening days,
defying the times, boxing the air.

Development

This duck will always touch
the surface of this dark
brackish pool, and, as it were,
freeze on digesting.
About the pit all trees
are strangely bare, no bird stays.

Around this ploughed-up field
grass is yellowed now
as if autumn came months early
and the path has dried hard.
Skylarks, once homed here,
are exiled to the wilderness beyond.

Our bushes hold on to
their late spring singers
till man's constructions plough on,
making wildlife an invader.
Meadow song is sacrificed
for car radios and unbridled iPods.

Blind development edges its stone-deaf cause
in corridors that accommodate no life.

On Environment

Forgive us that we build
and build again
upon my house
and snatch up more meadow.

Forgive us that our cars
are many here
and churn out
pollutants on the countryside.

Forgive us for the paper
that we unnecessarily
use to write these words,
which bring more trees to felling.

Forgive us that we have
to leave this land
many times a year,
though ozone depletes through us.

Forgive us that the centre
of our little worlds
is us, failing others
in our duty to this lovely world.

Where forgiveness is easy,
memory of wrongs done
soon fades away
and error is revisited.

The Island That Is a Town

It retreats
away from enemy lines
of junctioned motorways
and confluenced rivers
where land identifies
as tree, roof – then nothing.

Upon its termite hillock
it nestles snugly lapped
and washed afresh each day
by rushing, gushing flow
that leaves no stone unturned
nor car without its daily rinse.

Rising, surrounding
from every side, water
is always omnipresent
but no drop remains to drink.
The finger of disease waiting
lies just a touch beyond.

Vole

Here there are few voles now –
few to send droppings rolling
on down the bank;
their beady eyes showing with
drenched whiskers along the waterline
unhurried by a surge of water.
The minks had arrived,
gnashing their way
along the river, leaving
that tragic evidence of plunder.
But they didn't stay –
like Vikings they moved off
and away into the night,
seeking another kill.
Then man came along –
clearing, dredging, piping
but without music
other than the whine
of functional machinery
impacting the riverbank.
They too went, leaving nothing
but the emptiness of displacement.

Death of a Lake

We hadn't expected carnival
nor wild tangos of feathers
flashed around seductively,
but that absence of gulls
shrieking their hullabaloos
and the sole migrant grebe
diving out its own wake
was not the sight to stir us.

Stiff fins of fiercest pike
sailed the water's surface
like ancient wooden craft
without their sails,
drifting beyond the interest
of aerial scavengers
like ships of death bound
on their final voyage.

The wind gusted suddenly
and left that stinging scent
on skin and bleary eyes
that answers causal mysteries.
Somewhere unseen, uncaring hands
tipped their debris effluence
into a lively, cheerful stream
and sentenced life to death.

Elemental Pull

The lure of desert's
shifting sands evokes
strange shadow forms
that draw us in as dusk arrives.

The gaunt, still forest's
winter trees entice
us to explore their lair
and smell the musty scent of bark.

The grandeur of mountain's
sunny snow-capped summit
holds us breathless in gaze
and wish to touch such fragile form.

The call of the sea
shifting through its wildest moods
calls us home to ancient times
before the sun drops down on empty shores.

Butterflies

Through a gathering
of waving leaves
that alternate a glossy brilliance
with the matt of clouds,
through the canopy's cavities
that permit brief glimpses
of wandering wings,
our eyes fix dizzy
on a kaleidoscope
of changing forms.

A dash of white
or a thin-veined line
holds firm our gaze
until it slips from view;
and yet as we scan
in hope beyond the screen
we almost miss our quarry
sipping water by our feet.
How like us they like to wander
round each challenge,
seeking the optimum
that offers what we want.

Dawn Hunt

Hunter O'Driscoll
has shot his lead
far and high away
with fine puffs of smoke
into the pale misty cloth
that decks the boggy table.

A hundred geese or more
rise cackling loud
at his blindness –
though the error's not his –
and that extra chance
for them and dabbling ducks.

All is still now
by lake's murky margins
as the water gathers itself
in like a cryptic clan
excluding this alien
treading cold water in.

Dawn's inspiration rising
was not his this time,
nor the hopes
of a calm stealth's cull:
nature's curtain closets
around him keeping its secrets.

Panda

The sign of the logo
there for protection,
a peaceful creature,
thoughtful in his bamboo chew
and searching out
those vital nutrients.

Around him his world
is cropped like
tangled hair hanging
as a nuisance.

Stripped of his landscape
he is reduced to a tundra
of increased deprivation.
He takes the blame,
deemed weak by the potent
when he is merely vulnerable.

Somewhere in their atolls
of loose-connected power
the decision-makers
sit down together
and reassign the unsustainable
to unsupportable – unnecessary.

Tapiola

(The god of the forest in Finnish folklore)

I know a land
where lakes lie always deep
behind their swaying screens
of scented pines and tinted larch.
The waters are immobile
like reflected glass,
set as though for ever
in a postcard frame.

Anglers casting lines,
waiting for a catch,
will wait eternally
in the same still pose.
And yet the scene
begins to change
as mellow, tranquil air
absorbs fresh currents
as if guided firmly
by unerring, abstract force.

Conifers capture quick the mood
and lilt and swing
to the new rhythms
swirling on in from other climes.
Glass becomes serrated
as waves record their impact
on the brief, rocky shores
where ducks glide in for shelter.

The moods of the forest
now vary by each hour
as airborne eagles try
their skills to balance
on each shifting thermal
like edgy trapeze artists
and peer on through
the gliding, hanging clouds
to peering, pointing admirers
watching from below.

The hand that drives
these days of battling winds
knows that its time is short
till autumn meets it once again.
Divers, now newly landed,
harbour in the arbour
of bushy overhangs
and wail out eerie salutations.
Crossbills chip, grate and excavate
all day for seed, storing up
a larder for all demands
of the longer days to come.

Across the lakeland
there is the growing sense
that no winds can deflect
the course that nature takes
towards the peace of summer days,
the stilling of vernal winds.
The forest sighs its gentle peace
like the fine plucked strings
of violins, finding those last chords
before the note of silence.

Methane Labyrinths

We are the blind,
thread-feeling our ways
down tentacled labyrinths
that flatter but entangle;
our leaders share the blindness.
They lost the only eye
they might have kept
when they sold off vision.
Now we flounder on
in dim, damp passages
inhaling the daily increase
of methane we've released.
Captive of our planning
and decisions, now regretted,
we face the staring consequence
of resources ravaged by us.